You Know You're a Herper*...

WHEN YOU DREAM IN GREEN

*Reptile and amphibian lover

Compiled and Edited by
Allen & Anita Salzberg

A HerpArts Book

HerpArts Books
c/o A. Salzberg / 67-87 Booth Street
Flushing, NY 11375

Visit HerpArts.com for
gifts for reptile and amphibian lovers

Library of Congress Catalog
Card Number: 2004104376

ISBN: 0-9753235-0-4

Thanks to Tony Gamble for the
cover photo of *Corallus caninus* and
to Jim Van Abbema for editing.

Second Printing

Printed in the United States of America

Other books by
Allen & Anita Salzberg:

Confessions of a Turtle Wife
by Anita Salzberg
Hats Off Books

Available at:
Turtlewife.com
Amazon.com
and **HerpArts.com**

Turtles
by Anita Baskin-Salzberg
& Allen Salzberg

An exciting introduction
to turtles for kids ages 8 to 12.
Available at **HerpArts.com**

TABLE OF CONTENTS

INTRODUCTION

This book is about herpers: people who love and go to extraordinary lengths to study and/or keep snakes, frogs, lizards, and turtles.

(For those new to the subject, the term "herper" is derived from "herpetology," the branch of zoology that deals with reptiles and amphibians.)

It is a given that herpers are crazy in love with herps. They often risk life, limb, home, and marriage to study, breed, or keep reptiles and amphibians as pets.

Herpers shell out ridiculous sums for food, housing, and medical care for their animals, keep mice, worms, and bugs (i.e., herp food) in the fridge, may spend more time with their herps than with their families, and must fend off questions like, "You bought a pet...*what?* And it cost....*what?*", "Why can't you just get a cat?", and, "What do you mean...*you can't find it?!*"

Herpers know they're crazy, that they've crossed the line of an acceptable level of interest in, well, anything.

This book is a compendium of what herpers have to say for and about themselves. And what they have to say is hilarious, touching, occasionally sad, and often joyful.

As Beverly Hale of Chesterfield, Michigan, wrote: "Things sure do change when you become a herper."

As you read along, see if you don't agree.

* * * * * *

You will notice that while many contributors chose to have their names appear with their entries, others wished to remain anonymous.

We thank each and every one for their contributions, with special thanks to Pam Brzezinski of Mukwonago, Wisconsin, for her submission, "You know you're a herper when...you dream in green," that we've adapted for our title.

We hope you enjoy the book. We had a wonderful time compiling it.

Herpingly yours,
Allen & Anita Salzberg

HERP FOOD IN THE FRIDGE

You Know You're A Herper When...

...your freezer trays look like furry sausages; they're really frozen mice.
—Kathy Doyle, Maple Shade, NJ

...freezer space taken up by steak seems wasted.

...you have more than one freezer, but only one is used for *your* food.
—Rick Bradley, Lawrenceville, GA

You know you're a herper when...

...half of your refrigerator is taken
up by hibernating herps.
—Justin Reeves, St Joseph, MO

...the best fruits and veggies in the
fridge aren't for humans.

...every leftover container in your
fridge is filled with some kind
of bug or worm.
—Kathy Doyle, Maple Shade, NJ

...you panic if you get low
on bugs in the fridge.

...guests shriek when they
open your fridge.

...the chicken you take
out of the freezer tastes
a bit like "mouse."

BUGS AND CRICKETS

You know you're a herper when...

...bugs are welcome in your house.
—*Beverly Hale, Chesterfield, MI*

...your cat spends the nights
hunting your escaped crickets.
—*Zsuzsanna Horváth, Budapest, Hungary*

...you are deathly afraid of cockroaches,
and now you raise them.
—*Maria McArther, Caseyville, IL*

You know you're a herper when...

...you try food designed
for crickets just
to see how it tastes.

...you find yourself wondering, if
crickets are so good for herps,
why don't people eat crickets, too?
—*Rick Bradley, Lawrenceville, GA*

...you willingly let spiders set up shop in
your house to catch escaped
fruit flies and crickets.
—*Barbie Heid, West Haven, CT*

...you know the nutritional
content of bugs.

You know you're a herper when...

...you'll eat junk food, but "buy healthy"
for your crickets.
—*Barbie Heid, West Haven, CT*

...you find crickets and cricket parts all
over your house, but nowhere near
where you keep the crickets.
—*Maria McArther, Caseyville, IL*

...you turn off the lights and there are
more loose crickets chirping
inside than outside.
—*Lori Green, Merrick, NY*

...You can't sleep *without* the sound
of chirping crickets.
—*Maria McArther, Caseyville, IL*

AT THE SUPERMARKET

You know you're a herper when...

...you think nothing of spending more
per pound on rodents and bugs
than good steak costs.
—Keith Pahlke, Juneau, AK

...you live on Ramen noodles for a week
after spending the grocery money on
rodents for your snakes.

...the reptile grocery bill is bigger
than yours, and you don't care.

You know you're a herper when...

...you transform conventional,
pre-printed shopping lists to:
-Pinkies
-Fuzzies
-Mice
-Crickets
-Baby Food
-Pinheads
-Fruit Flies
—Barbie Heid, West Haven, CT

...you divide your groceries into people
and reptile purchases.
—Rick Bradley, Lawrenceville, GA

...you buy vegetables at the store and
you don't know what they're called.
—Beverly Hale, Chesterfield, MI

You know you're a herper when...

...you buy dandelions and mustard
greens at the grocery store, but no one
in your family eats them.

...you are overheard at the bait shop
asking for three dozen large juicy night
crawlers because your "kids" are picky
eaters and only like the big ones.

...the supermarket checkout lady asks
the age of your baby because you are
buying jars of baby food. You explain
that they're for your geckos.
She looks at you like you are nuts.
—Sue Field, Poughkeepsie, NY

You know you're a herper when...

...a fellow shopper in the supermarket
produce aisle asks for your recipe
for the dandelion greens you are
buying, and you admit that you
haven't got one.

... you first say, "I can't believe this
price for frozen rats!"
—G. Moore, Short Hills, NJ

FEEDING HERPS

You know you're a herper when...

...making salad for your iguana,
it's one piece for Mommy (me),
one for baby, two for Mommy....
—*Maria McArther, Caseyville, IL*

...you think of little Pomeranians
as snake food.

...you start using your toaster oven
as a "pinkie defroster."

You know you're a herper when...

...you'll drink tap water, but buy spring
water for your herps.
—Barbie Heid, West Haven, CT

...fast food involves the use of a
microwave and frozen mice.
—Michael Burroughs, Las Vegas, NV

...other people tell you what kind of pets
they have and you respond with,
"My snake could eat that!"

...you feed the herps
before the kids.

You know you're a herper when...

...you're elated to discover
termites near your house.
—Barbie Heid, West Haven, CT

...your wife screams that there's
a mouse in the bathroom, and you
are happy because you don't need
to buy food for your snake.
—Ezra Rosenbluth, Rosh HaAyn, Israel

...your monitor lizards eat more shrimp
and salmon than you do.
—Maria McArther, Caseyville, IL

You know you're a herper when...

...the work you put into the salads
you make for your family is nothing
compared with the work you put
into your bearded dragons' salad.
—Sue Field, Poughkeepsie, NY

...you get the same feeling of
satisfaction watching your bearded
dragons attack their greens as you
would watching your kids
at the dinner table.
—Sue Field, Poughkeepsie, NY

...your weekly ritual is neither Monday
night football, nor sorting through bills:
You make fruit fly cultures.
—Barbie Heid, West Haven, CT

You know you're a herper when...

...your box turtle gets first pick
of the first organic
strawberry crop you grow.

...you call friends and ask,
"Can I bum a few mice off of ya?"
—*Barbie Heid, West Haven, CT*

...you get excited when a co-worker
says they have a "mouse problem" and
you offer to take all they can catch.
—*Keith Pahlke, Juneau, AK*

You know you're a herper when...

...to insure you've fed every herp, you
start at the top shelf of each rack, and
begin: "No (incubator), yes, yes, yes, no
(in for rehab and tubing), yes, yes,"
until you've covered
all four walls of the room.
You devised this method after you
bagged and stored the day's food and
then discovered a hopeful-looking turtle
that you've overlooked.

SMILE FOR THE CAMERA!

You know you're a herper when...

...you show people your photo album of snakes the way most people show off their children's baby pictures.

...showing off pictures of your kids, you hear questions like, "Who's the little green guy?"

...you have more pictures of herps on your hard disk drive then you do pictures of your family.

You know you're a herper when...

...the only reason you want a digital
camera for Christmas is so you can take
pictures of your herps.

...your photo brag book contains more
pictures of your reptiles than
of your kids.
—*Sue Field, Poughkeepsie, NY*

DATING...WITH HERPS

You know you're a herper when...

...you ditch a boring date because you have to "spray your tanks."
—*Barbie Heid, West Haven, CT*

...you and your boyfriend break up, but you make sure that you have visitation rights to his prehensile tailed skink.
—*Christine Plesnicher, Cleveland, OH*

...while on a date, you stop to catch a rattlesnake crossing the road.
—*Steven Fox, Austin, TX*

You know you're a herper when...

...while still in school, you start to ask a
young lady on a first date. As you stand
there trying to be charming, you spy a
large toad off to your right.
In mid-sentence, you run over to see
what kind it is. Your date-to-be
speechlessly stares at you as you play
with your new amphibian friend. You
eventually ask her out. Things don't
work out between you, but you do still
love toads.

...you realize that frogs and turtles have
better personalities than most guys,
especially in a college town.
—*Krystal Davidson, Stillwater, OK*

MARRIED...WITH HERPS

You know you're a herper when...

...your spouse wishes he'd grow a shell
on his back so he'd get the same
preferential treatment as your turtles.

...your wife no longer notices all the
dead mice in the freezer.

...you say to your wife when mice are in
the kitchen, "Why are you screaming?
You never do this when you find
your son's food on the floor."
—*Ezra Rosenbluth,*
Rosh HaAyn, Israel

...your hubby doesn't like your reptiles
and other animals and you have a zoo:
cats, dogs, guinea pigs, ferrets, frogs,
snakes, turtles, and more.
Luckily, your husband says that the
things that make you an animal lover
also make you so good to him.
—*Beverly Hale, Chesterfield, MI*

...your lizards start getting more cuddle
time then your husband.
—*Penny Barnes, Winnipeg,
Manitoba, Canada*

...you run right past your husband and
kids to kiss your iguana when you
get home from work.

You know you're a herper when...

...you find yourself using radios in the
field to talk with your wife, because
photographing herps severely reduces
your walking speed relative to hers.
—*Victor Loehr, IJsselstein, Netherlands*

...you hesitate when your wife declares,
"Either they go or I go!"
—*R. Bonnett, Birdsboro, PA*

...you tell a fellow turtle pal that you're
getting divorced. He replies, "Hmm,
trading the wife for turtles.
Now that's a good deal."

You know you're a herper when...

...your final decision on which girlfriend
to marry is the one who will hold
the snake bag for you.
—Kevin Dees, Wharton, TX

You know *your wife* is a herper when...
...you call her to say you've NEARLY
been bitten by a female timber rattler
while trying to photograph it and her
reply is monotone and something like,
"That's nice dear, you know you should
have tried to take the picture
from her good side."
—Jack Kottwitz, Pickerington, OH

TV AND HERPS

You know you're a herper when...

...while watching your favorite movie, *Jurassic Park*, you revel in the idea that humans are made of meat.

...TIVO is set to record any show containing the word "Reptile."

...you are clueless to world events, but always know what's on Animal Planet, Discovery Safari, and National Geographic.
—*Barbie Heid, West Haven, CT*

You know you're a herper when...

...Animal Planet does a show on reptiles
and you realize you live with half the
animals they are describing.
—Lori Green, Merrick, NY

...you speed dial seven friends during a
30-second commercial to tell them it
features a sulcata tortoise.
—Lori Green, Merrick, NY

...you always have Mark Ochea,
Jeff Corwin, or Steve Irwin
on your TV.

HERP LOVE

You know you're a herper when...

...the last thing you do before going to
bed is check on all your snakes to make
sure they're safely "tucked in."

...a sale on dead mice
makes your day.

...you hope you come across
snakes when hiking.

You know you're a herper when...

...you are delighted at not only holding a
fat toad in your hands, but at hearing
its release call as it pees on you.
—*Nettie Lambert, Corvallis, OR*

...your friends go to art galleries and
critique the placement of subject
matter. You go to the zoo and say,
"Well, I woulda put the rocks here..."
—*Barbie Heid, West Haven, CT*

...you refuse to use a Band-Aid
because the claw mark you just got
was too cool not to show it off.
—*Lori Green, Merrick, NY*

...seeing a needlessly killed herp
makes you very sad.

You know you're a herper when...

...you try to persuade your boss that
a hatching tortoise egg is a good
reason to skip a working day.
—*Victor Loehr,*
IJsselstein, Netherlands

...you call in sick to work so you
can stay home to look
for a missing snake.

...you find snakes, venomous
or otherwise, while hiking,
and move them to a safe place,
rather than killing them or
running off in terror.

You know you're a herper when...

...your husband hands you your first
tortoise (a sulcata) on Valentine's day,
it pees all over you, but you don't care;
you're in love.

...you hide a snake in an aquarium for
over a year, feeding it goldfish on
the sly, because your parents
won't let you have a snake.

...you're the only one of your friends
who still goes down to the pond for
hours on end with a net looking
for herps.

...you first say: "Oh good! The skin
on her face finally fell off!"

You know you're a herper when...

...you start each day turning on
all the tank lights and saying,
"Hello babies," or, "Hi guys,"
before you wake up your kids.
—*Bettina M. Sailer, North Aurora, IL*

...in the morning, checking on
the lizard comes before coffee.

...your good night kiss is from
a Mali *Uromastyx*.

...you honestly think toads
are the most adorable creatures
on the planet.

You know you're a herper when...

...you can walk into a specialty reptile
shop and not think it smells funny.
—Rick Bradley, Lawrenceville, GA

...you've always been fascinated
with puddles, pools, ponds, and
what's wiggling within.
—Connie Ranson, Farmington, PA.

...you are happy to see poop.
—Rick Bradley, Lawrenceville, GA

...you've fawned over a snake
as if it were a puppy.

You know you're a herper when...

...you own a field guide to reptiles of a
country you are not likely to ever visit.
Rick Bradley, Lawrenceville, GA

...before going to buy mice, you wiggle
your fingers (and try to make them look
like a mouse) in front of your snake's
cage to see if she is hungry.

...you have an entire series of shelves
devoted to frog miniatures.

...every T-shirt you own
has something to do with reptiles.
—Lori Green, Merrick, NY

...someone yells "Snake!", and you're
the only one running toward it.

...the hardest thing in your life is
losing two Chinese water dragons
that meant the world to you.
—*Maria McArther, Caseyville, IL*

...you watch your mom lose her beloved
chameleon and you cry together.
—*Maria McArther, Caseyville, IL*

HOUSEKEEPING
AND HERPS

You know you're a herper when...

... you have better Tupperware
for "soaking" herps than you
have for your food.
—*Beverly Hale, Chesterfield, MI*

...you begin buying bagged soil
for your reptile instead
of for your flowers.

You know you're a herper when...

...you own more thermometers
and hygrometers than you
do eating utensils.
—Barbie Heid, West Haven, CT

...you have no place to display your
knick-knacks because every flat
surface in your house is covered
with snake enclosures.

...you've told visitors, "Please
excuse the house!" but your
herp tanks are spotless.
—Barbie Heid, West Haven, CT

...the first thing you think about
during a power outage is keeping
your snakes warm.

You know you're a herper when...

...the longest part of your morning
routine is making sure
all the water is clean.
—*Sarah Richard, Minneapolis, MN*

...buying house paint, here's how you
find yourself trying to describe the
color you want to the
paint department guy:
"You know, that shade of blue,
like a Standing's day gecko?"
—*Barbie Heid, West Haven, CT*

...you never throw away small boxes,
because they make good hideaways.
—*Barbie Heid, West Haven, CT*

You know you're a herper when...

...rodent maintenance replaces
the chore of lawn care.
—*Michael Burroughs, Las Vegas, NV*

...you are always watching for sales on
light bulbs, electrical timers and
multi-socket power strips.
—*Keith Pahlke, Juneau, AK*

...you fold your wash and find two or
more pillow cases or snake bags still
stuffed into your pants pockets.

...you have a ton of turkey basters
labeled "reptiles only."
—*Barbie Heid, West Haven, CT*

You know you're a herper when...

...you own lots of plastic storage boxes,
but can't use them because they
all have holes cut in them.
—Carolyn Quinn Renier, Kerrville, TX

...you've had to move the refrigerator,
not to vacuum the dust bunnies,
but to find an escaped snake.
—Barbie Heid, West Haven, CT

HOME SWEET HOME

You know you're a herper when...

...you are the proud owner of ALL the
leaky aquariums in the neighborhood.
—*Thomas McNeil, Elizabethton, TN*

...you have a baby pool in
your backyard but no baby.

...there is a turtle pond in
your kitchen, and lizards have a
spot on your couch.

You know you're a herper when...

...with all the UV lights in your
home, you essentially have
your own tanning bed.
—Maria McArther, Caseyville, IL

...your iguana's setup costs the
equivalent of one month's
house payment.
—Maria McArther, Caseyville, IL

...your cat sleeps next to the ceramic
heat emitter on top of your
snake's cage.

...people start to refer
to your room
as "Lizard Land."

You know you're a herper when...

...you have to explain to the pool
guy why there is a tree branch
soaking in the deep end.

...your reptiles get a bigger
room than you do.

...your bedroom is 10 to 15 degrees
warmer than the rest of the house due
to the heat from all the basking bulbs.

...you don't have room to move around
in your bedroom because of
all the herp enclosures.

You know you're a herper when...

...you buy a special vacuum cleaner
that removes aspen shavings
from the rugs.

...the dust bunnies under your furniture
are mixed with snake shed.

...you have to warn visitors about the
turtles in the sink and bathtub.
—Kathy Doyle, Maple Shade, NJ

...you tell your children their bathtub
belongs to the bugs now.

...the power bill goes up $50 a month,
and you don't complain.

You know you're a herper when...

...you tell visitors to wear or bring
shorts and a T-shirt to your house,
even in the dead of winter, because
of the tropical temperatures
and humidity.

...the only pillow cases on your
pillows are the holey ones that won't
hold a snake.

...your yard looks like someplace
where National Geographic
could film a TV special.
—*Lori Green, Merrick, NY*

You know you're a herper when...

...you begin buying new furniture
so the old stuff can be
made into cages.

...you realize you no longer view
furniture as a necessity or comfort
item, but as a future vivarium
for your water dragon.

YOU HAVE
HOW MANY HERPS?!

You know you're a herper when...

...you have 14 turtles, they all
have names, but you can't remember
who is who.

...you can recite all of your snakes'
names, but you can't remember how
many snakes you actually have.

...you consider moving your bed
out of your room to have
more area for tanks.

You know you're a herper when...

...you tell your husband you need a bigger house because you have no more space to display your turtle knick-knacks.

...you stand in your bedroom doorway trying to figure out which pieces of furniture you can do without, in order to make room for more enclosures to hold your ever-growing collection.
—*Laura S., Fullerton, CA*

...you catch yourself looking at fine antique cabinets ($600 and up) and thinking, "Hmm, wonder how many snakes I can fit into that?"

...Your family doesn't want to let you leave home with money in your pocket.
—*Zsuzsanna Horváth, Budapest, Hungary*

You know you're a herper when...

...your family hears from you for
the 100th time that this lizard (snake,
turtle, etc.) will be the last.
—Zsuzsanna Horváth, Budapest, Hungary

...asked how many pets you have you say
"Only 70, but I have only one cat."
—Sarah Richard, Minneapolis, MN

...you count and are forced to
admit that anyone with 10 frogs,
several salamanders, 7 turtles, and
12 lizards is indeed a herper.
Angela Steffke, Lincoln Park, MI

...you look around and realize that there
are more reptiles in your computer
room than most pet stores have in
their entire reptile inventory.
—Cristina Loder, Powell, TN

FRIENDS AND FAMILY
AND HERPS

You know you're a herper when...

...your in-laws refuse to come into the
house after you make them
watch a snake swallow a rodent.

...your sister-in-law screams and drops
a tub of butter she's taken from
the fridge when she realizes it
is actually a tub of worms.
—*Lori Green, Merrick, NY*

You know you're a herper when...

You know you are
a *herping family* when...
...you bring home an alligator and all
your kids want to know is when
will dinner be ready and what
are you serving.
—Lori Green, Merrick, NY

...your parents refuse to come
into your room for fear
of getting salmonella.

...nobody visits your house
because of "what's in there..."
—Barbie Heid, West Haven, CT

You know you're a herper when...

...visitors are horrified to see a gecko
roaming the walls, and you explain,
"Oh, he's for cricket control..."
—Barbie Heid, West Haven, CT

...you cancel plans to go out with
your friends to stay home
and find the loose snake.
—Lori Green, Merrick, NY

...your "kids" are your eight
lizards and snakes.
—Maria McArther, Caseyville, IL

...your friends and relatives would
rather come to your house
than go to the zoo.

You know you're a herper when...

...you visit friends or relatives and
spend the day flipping rocks
and logs in their backyard.
—*Barbie Heid, West Haven, CT*

NEIGHBORS AND HERPS

You know you're a herper when...

...you don't get any trick-or-treaters on Halloween because everyone in the neighborhood knows you keep snakes.

...you spot kids peeping in your windows to see if they can see your snakes.

...your neighbors constantly complain about moss popping up in their yard, but you think, "That'd be cool in my tank."
—Barbie Heid, West Haven, CT

You know you're a herper when...

...any one of any age greets you in public
as "the snake/turtle/lizard/frog man."
—*Rick Bradley, Lawrenceville, GA*

...you stop inviting the neighbors in
because you're afraid they will find you
have a "dangerous" garter snake and
agitate to have you removed
from the neighborhood.

...every kid you know has brought
you a frog, snake, lizard,
or turtle to identify.
—*Jim Trostle, Columbus GA*

You know you're a herper when...

...you find yourself explaining to the
neighbours that the cricket sounds in
their house did not originate from
crickets that escaped from your lizard
breeding facilities, but from
crickets that occur naturally
in the middle of town.
— *Victor Loehr,*
IJsselstein, Netherlands

MOMS AND HERPS

You know you're a herper when...

...your mom knows exactly what to do
when she encounters an escaped snake
in the house—and does it!

...you enlist your mother to bring back
some chameleons in her luggage because
she happens to be flying in from the
same city as the reptile dealer.

You know you're a herper when...

...your mother, who doesn't know the
difference between a salamander
and a lizard, says enthusiastically,
"This is a *Uromastyx!*"
when she sees a *Uromastyx.*
—*Zsuzsanna Horváth, Budapest, Hungary*

...your son, explaining to his high
school friends about his mother's
stopping at every creek along
the road and "herpin,'" says,
"But she's a GOOD kind-a crazy!"
—*Carol A. Pollio, Falmouth, VA*

You know you're a herper when...

...while out herpin' with your 17-year-
old son, turning over rocks along
a stream bank, getting muddy
and wet, he says, "You know, Mom,
that's what I love about you—
you're not a wuss!"
—Carol A. Pollio, Falmouth, VA

...your mom, who has previously
declared that she hates snakes,
asks for one for her own.
—Jay Duenkel, Fulton, KS

...your mother (grandmother in my case)
can never find any of the clean
pillowcases she's just washed.
—Thomas McNeil, Elizabethton, TN

You know you're a herper when...

...you're in the seventh grade. Your
grandmother stays at your house all day
to be there when you and your brother
return from school. Before lunch one
day, you're called to the principal's
office, and your mother hurries you
home to help with an "emergency."
Your grandmother is outside waiting for
you. There is "something" in the kitchen
stove. It is your pet garter snake,
who has poked her head out
from the pot drawer.

You know you're a herper when...

...you're ten years old, and you look
down between your feet to see a
massasauga clearly close enough
to immediately bite either leg.
Your immediate reaction is,
"Cool! My first *Sistrurus* ever!"
Your mother, standing nearby, faints.
—*Don Pitts, Urbana IL*

KIDS AND HERPS

You know you're a herper when...

...as a kid, you won't put a frog down a little girl's dress because you're afraid you won't get the frog back.
—Kevin Enge, Havana, FL

...you are a kid and your mum yells out, "What are these lizards doing in your bed?" And you respond: "Hibernating."

...at least once every summer, while working on your aunt's farm, you capture a toad and chase her with it.

You know you're a herper when...

...you must stay after school to write,
"I will not bring snakes
and frogs to class."
—*Barbie Heid, West Haven, CT*

...you learn the word "herpetology"
in the 5th grade.

...you're nine or ten years old.
Every Wednesday a different camper
in your YMCA camp group gets to
choose the activity for the afternoon;
you choose lizard hunting.
—*M. Welker, Gainesville, FL*

You know you're a herper when...

...in middle school, instead of playing
with makeup and starting to chase guys,
you are still chasing frogs.

...having a bullfrog dropped into your
bathing suit at Boy Scout camp evokes
the response, "Wow, where
did you find it?"

...you ask your parents for a tortoise
as a Bar Mitzvah gift.
—*Allen Salzberg, Forest Hills, NY*

...you grab a snake, it whips around to
bite you, and you hold on anyway.
You are eight.

You know you're a herper when...

...you are around eight, living in the
foothills of east Tennessee on your
family's farm. Your granddaddy calls
you and your sisters outside.
He's run over a snake with the lawn
mower, and a frog has popped halfway
out of the dead snake's mouth.
Your sisters start to shriek;
you are amazed and captivated.
—Rebecca B. Smith,
Kennedy Space Center, FL

...at an early age, rubbing a toad's belly,
then waiting to see how long it
takes to right itself can hold
your attention for hours.

You know you're a herper when...

...at around seven, you are bitten by a
garter snake in your yard. From then on,
you learn everything about every
snake you can find.

...at seven, you find yourself riding
public transportation sunburned,
exhausted, and reeking of pond muck,
garter snake musk, and frog mucus. And
you realize that this is way more fun
than playing soccer.

...as a child, you are bewildered by
the wild accusations made
against the perfectly innocent
snakes you have met.

You know you're a herper when...

...your dad says there's a snake loose in
the house. After a few minutes of
searching, you find it under the couch
and manage to grab the back of it.
The snake swings its head around and
latches onto your arm.
You've been a herper ever since you
pried your arm out of its mouth.

...you are nine years old and your father
brings you to a hospital to identify what
kind of snake has bitten someone.
—*Bill Summer, Rome, GA*

...at around nine years old, you put a
toad on your tongue
to impress your friends.
—*Barbara Wales, La Grande, OR*

You know you're a herper when...

...in high school, you can pronounce
Latin better than most of the Latin II
students and the faculty call on you
whenever a herp (or bug—you can
handle all the creepy crawlies) is found
in the school, like a garter snake that
falls out of the ceiling onto
one of the teachers.

...at eleven, you undertake your first
mark-and-recapture study on the large
population of horned toads in the vacant
lot next to your house. You mark them
by painting their horns with red nail
polish. You work diligently at this, and
your efforts do not go unnoticed. One
day, the woman next door announces to
your mother that she has discovered
a new species of horned toad!

You know you're a herper when...

...you are just as excited at catching your first wild snake as you are at learning to ride a bike.

...you are four years old and realize that opening your animal picture book to the page with the snake on it will cause your grandmother to leave the room.

...you are a child and the local layperson naturalist, Mrs. Thompson, lets you hold the hellbender she has caught in the Allegheny River. This weird looking salamander that can glue your fingers together is all that is needed to "stick" herps in your mind.
—*Bill Gates, Madison, AL*

You know you're a herper when...

...you are happier carrying around your
pet snake than you are carrying around
your pet cat.

...you first hear your mother's voice
coming from an upstairs bedroom:
"Oh, boys, I found your snake!"
—*Edward I. Pollak, West Chester, PA*

...you beat up a neighborhood kid for
blowing up a frog with a firecracker.
—*Kevin Williams, North Fork, CA*

...you know that the best way to make
new friends in a new state is
to start a herp club.

You know you're a herper when...

...between around eight to twelve
years old, you get bit by just about
every snake or lizard you can catch,
and catch them anyway.
—*Kevin Williams, North Fork, CA*

...around 1955, the American Museum
of Natural History calls you and your
twin brother to acquire some live
turtles for their kids' exhibit.
—*Edward I. Pollak, West Chester, PA*

...As a three year old, you get to ride on
the back of a gopher tortoise that your
grandpa carved his initials onto when he
was a kid. But you won't let your three-
year-old daughter ride the same
tortoise (she weighed too much).

You know you're a herper when...

...you are six or so and your dad takes
you and your brother outside to point
out various plants and beasts. One day
while with him, you flip a half-rotten
sack lying on the ground. Underneath
are what you now know to be two blind
snakes. They get away and you don't get
a good look, but you are hooked on
herps for life.

...at three years old you go missing.
Your parents are sure you've been
kidnapped or lost, but you have merely
walked down the block to the "snake
lady's" house to see her corn snakes.
Eventually your parents get so used
to this that whenever they can't find
you, they know that's where you will be.
—*Laura Dixon, Brookings, SD*

...I knew my son and I were confirmed
herpers when he was almost three. We
were driving along singing *Old McDonald*
when he said, "Old McDonald had a
snake, with a hiss hiss here and a hiss
there." It broke me up so much I about
ran off the road laughing:

Old McDonald had a farm
ee ii ee ii o
and on this farm he had a snake

ee ii ee ii oo
with a hiss hiss here
and a hiss hiss there
and a hiss hiss everywhere
Old McDonald had a farm
ee ii ee ii oo

You know you're a herper when...

Old McDonald had a farm
ee ii ee ii o
and on this farm he had a rattlesnake
ee ii ee ii oo
with a rattle rattle here
and a rattle rattle there
and a rattle rattle everywhere
Old McDonald had a farm
ee ii ee ii oo

That was over thirty years ago. I guess
you could have a whole songbook with
toads croaking, frogs jumping,
salamanders slithering, and turtles
doing whatever turtles do best.
—Carl Lasher, San Antonio, TX

You know you're a herper when...

...you encounter a garter snake, most
likely a hatchling, at age 11. That little
snake is so cute, you know then
and there you have to get
to know snakes better.
—*Diane L. Smith, Everett, WA*

...at age four, you climb down into the
alligator pit at the Birmingham Zoo.
Your father sees you at the bottom of
the ladder and quietly but urgently
requests that you climb back out.
Your reply: "But, Daddy, he loves me!
Daddy, he loves me!"
You can be sure your parents never let
you out of their sight at the zoo again.
—*Nisa Rauschenberg, Tappan, NY*

GOING ABOVE AND BEYOND
FOR HERPS

You know you're a herper when...

...you're taking a bath and a missing
snake crawls out of the overflow drain.

...you are at an exceptional party
on a rainy day and all you can think
about is whether or not your turtle pool
will flood—and of course,
you leave the party.

You know you're a herper when...

...you hate long car rides but you'll drive
400 miles to a reptile show.

...you spend an extra 20 minutes getting
ready one morning trying to cover up a
snake bite on your face.

...you try to revive a lizard with
artificial respiration or CPR—and
succeed.

...you go out in a Texas tornado to
collect your turtles so you can take
them down to the basement with you.

You know you're a herper when...

...even though you broke your foot and
are on crutches, you still check on
your outdoor turtles.

...you dangle a mouse in front of your
python's face in just the right place so
she can strike at the mouse
and not bite you.

...you step on a nail and still manage
to grab the kingsnake.

...you spend $1000 to have a restaurant-
quality three-hole sink installed
in your herp room.
—*Sarah Richard, Minneapolis, MN*

You know you're a herper when...

...you jump out of a boat into a swamp in
your good clothes to catch
a water snake.

...you flip the canoe, lose all your gear,
and hold up a turtle
with excitement.

...you do not care that you must lay
still on your belly on top of an ant's
nest in order to get a unique photo
of a free-ranging lizard.
—*Victor Loehr,*
IJsselstein, Netherlands

You know you're a herper when...

83

...you find your mouth full of stinking aquarium water when siphoning out your turtle enclosures, and still continue keeping these creatures.
— Victor Loehr,
IJsselstein, Netherlands

...you have pneumonia and are supposed to be resting, and you just have to add onto and remodel your dragon's vivarium because you feel he needs more climbing room.

...you find yourself happily chest deep in alligator-infested waters.

You know you're a herper when...

...you have claw marks all
up and down your arms.
—Maria McArther, Caseyville, IL

...you are about eight and "collecting"
tadpoles in a backwater along a river in
California. The kid you are with tosses
a jar at you that hits you in the eye.
Your eye begins to bleed and swell.
Your friend, aghast, wants to leave.
You don't. You walk to the river, pick up
a flat rock that is cold from the water,
hold it to your eye and go back to
observing and collecting.
You probably use twenty rocks
on your eye that day.

You know you're a herper when...

...after fourteen scars, ten stitches,
multiple abrasions, and one severe bout
of diarrhea, courtesy of your iguana,
you still spend time each day preparing
a better salad for the iguana than you
have ever eaten in your life.
—Rick Bradley, Lawrenceville, GA

HERPS IN THE MIDDLE
OF THE ROAD

You know you're a herper when...

...you pull off the road to help a toad
or a turtle get across.

...you see a black rat snake crossing the
road. You jump out of your truck while
it's still moving to save the snake from
injury or death. You've forgotten that
no one is behind the wheel of your truck
as it's heading down the tarmac.

You know you're a herper when...

...you talk a state trooper into stopping
traffic on a busy road to rescue
a stranded turtle.
—*Steven Fox, Austin, TX*

...you get out of your car to chase
frogs out of the road.
—*Jim Trostle, Columbus GA*

...you realize that you now stop to LOOK
at road kills, rather than avoid them.
—*Carol A. Pollio, Falmouth, VA*

...you've been repeatedly honked at for
driving 5 mph on rainy nights.

You know you're a herper when...

...you drive 25 miles an hour
to avoid hitting snakes and frogs
on the highway—in Texas.
Rosalee Addis, Venice, FL

...you jog six miles to the nearest phone
because you've gotten out of the car to
help a turtle out of the middle of the
road and locked your keys in the car
with it still running.

GETTING BIT BY A HERP

You know you're a herper when...

...your snake is swallowing your finger
and you don't know what to do.

...you sit around the table during dinner
and compare bite marks and
claw scratches like veterans
comparing battle scars.
—Lori Green, Merrick, NY

... you've been seriously injured in
pursuit of a salamander.

You know you're a herper when...

...you realize that you don't mind at all being bit; in fact, you find yourself letting herps bite because it seems to make them feel better after being caught, picked up, and scrutinized. You even talk to them while they're biting and praise them for being so fierce. Your students think you're completely nuts.

...having pondered for years what to get a tattoo of, it hits you: The first snake that bites you will get a tribute on your body.
—*Lindsay Davis Funk, Maryland*

You know you're a herper when...

...as a sub-teen you are walking through a vacant lot after a ball game and see kids about to shoot a garter snake with a BB gun. You run over, push the gun aside, and reach down for the snake, which, of course, bites you.

...the scorpion clinging to the bottom of the rock you've just stuck your fingers under looking for a reptile makes you create some new word combinations.

VACATIONS AND HERPS

You know you're a herper when...

...while vacationing at the Grand Canyon,
everybody else is looking at the view;
you're down in the rocks
chasing lizards.

...you talk to your college buddies about
how excited you are about the things
you will do and see on your spring break
and summer trips to Florida—and
they have nothing to do with
partying and drinking.
—*Robert Jadin, Tehlequah, OK*

You know you're a herper when...

...your wife suggests a possible place to
vacation and you check your field guide
to see what kind of reptiles
you will find there.

...you plan a vacation in Florida and
don't even CONSIDER visiting
the Magic Kingdom.
—Rosalee Addis, Venice, FL

...while vacationing at a luxurious
destination, you spend $100 rebooking
your plane ticket after your caretaker
phones to say that a tortoise
egg is hatching.
— Victor Loehr,
IJsselstein, Netherlands

You know you're a herper when...

...you plan vacations around herping
and herp shows.
—Barbie Heid, West Haven, CT

...enjoying vacations gets difficult
away from your pals.

...you stop your car 1,000 times on a 100
mile trip thinking you are going to save
another turtle; most of the time you
end up removing another piece of big rig
retread from the road.
—Frederick Feldman, Elkins Park, PA

IN THE FIELD WITH HERPS

You know you're a herper when...

...you slog through a swamp wearing a
pair of leaky waders in 98 degree heat
with mosquitoes as big as dragonflies,
just to check your
PVC pipes for treefrogs.
—*Brian Bockhahn, Wake Forest, NC*

...at the age of 17, you realize that
finding a job that will allow you to
work with herps is a goal
to steadfastly pursue.

You know you're a herper when...

...your glove compartment is overflowing
with topo maps.

...you get really happy about it starting
to rain at night just as you
are going out to do fieldwork—
because tuatara like wet nights.

...you spend your Friday and Saturday
nights on the side of a road listening to
frogs (conducting calling frog surveys).

...your rear-view mirror decoration
is a fold-away snake hook.

You know you're a herper when...

...your favorite shoes are perpetually covered in mud and duct tape.

...you wage war with a coyote family that is trying to move into a gopher tortoise colony on your land.

...at age 27, you spend your summer nights cruising until 4 a.m. hoping to find just one more specimen of night snake; all the while listening to AC/DC at full blast in a desperately effort not to lapse into a sleep deprived coma. Then you do it all over again the following night.

You know you're a herper when...

...you refuse to allow a junked car to be
towed away until the gopher tortoise
that lives under it has moved
to a new burrow.

THE COMPUTER/INTERNET AND HERPS

You know you're a herper when...

...your Internet favorites list
of herp sites is longer than your
grocery list.

...you can't wait to read your e-mail,
to see what's up on the
snake/frog/gecko lists.
—*Barbie Heid, West Haven, CT*

You know you're a herper when...

...you realize you have more email from
other herpers than from any other
group of people you know.

...all your PC wallpaper is herp-related,
as are your cursors and folder icons.
—*Barbie Heid, West Haven, CT*

MAGAZINES AND BOOKS
AND HERPS

You know you're a herper when...

...in college, you rationalize sharing
someone else's course books and not
buying your own because of the
numerous herp books that
you can buy instead.
—Robert Jadin, Tehlequah, OK

...you rush to the mailbox
to get advertising flyers, not
because you care what's on sale,
but to line the snake cages.
—Barbie Heid, West Haven, CT

You know you're a herper when...

...you're more interested in
Reptiles Magazine than the *Sports
Illustrated Swim Suit Edition.*

...you own a book titled *101 Ways to
Satisfy Your Reptile.*

...you think a great read would be a book
titled *Reptile Medicine and Surgery.*
—Rick Bradley, Lawrenceville, GA

You know you're a herper when...

you misplace your car keys at least
once a day, but you always know exactly
where to find your field guide.

...you consider Peterson,
Conant, Collins, and Rossi to be
"great authors of our time."
—*Barbie Heid, West Haven, CT*

MAIL DELIVERY AND HERPS

You know you're a herper when...

...your UPS agent is afraid to ask you, "What's in the box?"

...the mailman/UPS guy knows you by name because of the fruit fly and cricket shipments you receive.
—Barbie Heid, West Haven, CT

You know you're a herper when...

...the FedEx delivery woman looks at you strangely as she hands you your monthly package of live crickets.

...the postal service learns to leave packages on your front steps instead of risking returning them to the post office for later pick up.

...Air Cargo employees begin to refer to you as "The Crocodile Hunter."

HOLIDAYS, BIRTHDAYS AND HERPS

You know you're a herper when...

...you buy Christmas presents for your herps (and wrap them).
—*Barbie Heid, West Haven, CT*

...you ask your family for money for Christmas to buy a large tank, and soon find yourself surrounded by 14 adult firebelly toads, the 17 hatchling firebelly toads they give birth to, and 2 anoles you've bought with the gift.
—*Bettina M. Sailer, North Aurora, IL*

You know you're a herper when...

...your favorite present is
"a really cool branch."

You've always known you were a
herper. From the time you were five or
six until, well...recent years...you've
checked every single Christmas
present for air holes.
You kept hoping that someone had
taken your many hints seriously.
—David G. Barker, Boerne, TX

...you sign birthday and holiday cards
with the names of all your herps.
—Barbie Heid, West Haven, CT

You know you're a herper when...

...your husband gets you a five-foot-
long python for Christmas—and
he's terrified of snakes.

...you receive an audio tape of Christmas
music (from a fellow herper) done by
croaking toads and frogs. Listening to
it, you try to identify the different
species croaking out "Jingle Bells"
and "Silent Night."
—Connie Ranson, Farmington, PA

...your Christmas, birthday, and
anniversary gift wish lists consist of
only new snakes for your collection.
Becky Willitts, Claremont, CA

You know you're a herper when...

... you receive a Tupperware tub full
of superworms as a Christmas gift
and you are delighted and grateful.

...your Santa wish list includes frozen
mice, terrarium plants,
and cricket treats.

...holiday shopping means finding a herp
show held during December.

...your friends and family say you are
the easiest person to shop for because
all they have to do is buy
a turtle knick-knack.

...the traditional garland on the family
Christmas tree is abandoned for shed
rattlesnake skins leftover from
a survey you did last summer.
—*R. Bonnett, Birdsboro, PA*

PET STORES AND HERPS

You know you're a herper when...

...you cruise pet stores instead
of the mall.

...you've explained to a pet store
manager that the "Eastern box turtle"
he's selling is actually a red-eared
slider.

...everyone at your local herp store
knows your name.

...you try to teach pet stores the "right
way" to take care of herps.
—*Jay Duenkel, Fulton, KS*

...pet store employees
refer customers with reptile
questions to *you.*

HERP HEALTH

You know you're a herper when...

...you're the weird one with the strange
pets at the vet's office.
—*Maria McArther, Caseyville, IL*

...you haven't been to the eye doctor in
years, but you religiously check your
snake's sheds for eyecaps.
—*Barbie Heid, West Haven, CT*

You know you're a herper when...

...you're unaware that a friend or family
member has a critical allergy to a food
ingredient, but you know that you
can't feed your iguana broccoli
because it gives him diarrhea.
—*Barbie Heid, West Haven, CT*

...your first male leopard gecko gets ill
and you take care of him like you take
care of your kids when they are
sick. You mix his bug slurry and freeze
it and spend hours feeding him—and
make your kids feed themselves.

HERP TALK

You know you're a herper when...

...you know the Latin names of all 36 of
your lizards and snakes.

...you know how to say *Uromastyx*.

...you're aware that a "boid"
is not a New York City pigeon.

...you do not automatically think "pizza"
when you hear the word "caecilian"
(legless amphibian).
—*Rick Bradley, Lawrenceville, GA*

You know you're a herper when...

...you can ask your friends if they have
herps, and they know you aren't talking
about venereal disease.
—Rick Bradley, Lawrenceville, GA

...you know the word for snake in several
languages just so your pets can have
"cool but educational" names.
—Rick Bradley, Lawrenceville, GA

...you know the definition
of the word "herp."
—Barbie Heid, West Haven, CT

GENERAL HERP CRAZINESS

You know you're a herper when...

...you start calling your herps terms
of endearment like Cutie,
Speed Bump, and Dot.

...you meet someone and your first
question is, "Are you afraid of snakes?"
rather than, "Hi, my name is..."
—Heidi Pfeifer, Pretoria, South Africa

You know you're a herper when...

...the first time you pick up a toad and
say (in that baby talk voice),
"Ohhhh, isn't he CUUUUUTE???"

...you have tips for people on how to
remove a snake from their arm.
—Rick Bradley, Lawrenceville, GA

...you go to a reptile show with your
eleven-year-old and you run into the
show faster than your kid because
you are SO EXCITED!
—Sue Field, Poughkeepsie, NY

...garter snake musk starts
to smell good.
—Kevin Enge, Havana, FL

You know you're a herper when...

...you bring your toad outside to
the garden "for a walk."
—*Barbie Heid, West Haven, CT*

...you're annoyed that poison arrow
frogs loose their toxicity in captivity.
—*Rick Bradley, Lawrenceville, GA*

...you make a slow motion digital movie
of your Russian tortoise prowling
through the garden eating to make it
look like an old black and white
Godzilla movie.

...clean stool sample results became
cause for celebration.

You know you're a herper when...

...you can't walk past a rock, log, or leaf
pile without turning it over looking
for salamanders—even if it's
in the middle of downtown.

...after taking care of an Argus monitor,
you're not too scared of anything.
—Maria McArther, Caseyville, IL

...the only way you can identify your car
in a large parking lot is your "I Brake
for Snakes" bumper sticker.

...you head-bob back at your
lizard (and win).

You know you're a herper when...

...as a senior in college, you are out at
night recording the mating calls of *Bufo
woodhouseii, Bufo americanus*, and their
hybrids while your friends are...well,
surely not recording toad calls.
—*Doug Holy, Washington, DC*

... you talk to your reptiles more
than to your friends.

...a little green creature with a white
mask of skin hanging off its
head is cute to you.

...you send out birth announcements
for a hatching.
—*Barbie Heid, West Haven, CT*

You know you're a herper when...

...you spend countless hours pondering
why frogs and toads do the
toe-tap when hunting food.
—Barbie Heid, West Haven, CT

...you get a 17" TV set specifically
for Charlie, your red-eared slider,
so he can watch Jerry Springer.
And you angle the set so Charlie on
his basking platform gets the
best view of the screen.
—Laurie Squire, Martinsville, NJ

...everyone brings their new puppies to
work, so you bring your iguana—and
actually hope for the same oohs
and ahhs from co-workers.
—Stephanie Marshall, Denair, CA

You know you're a herper when...

...you constantly buy the wrong size
clothing for your family as gifts, but
you can eyeball a frozen mouse and say,
"Oh, yeah, Stinky can eat that."
—*Barbie Heid, West Haven, CT*

...the moment the tattoo needle
hits your skin.
—*Lori Green, Merrick, NY*

...you don't keep cards people
send you, but you have
all of your snake's sheds.
—*Barbie Heid, West Haven, CT*

You know you're a herper when...

...you can clear half of a restaurant
simply by discussing feeding methods
over dinner with a herper friend.

...you pick up hitchhikers only if they
are carrying a stick with a
hook at the end.

...you are informed there is a snake on
your head and you answer,
"I know, I put it there."

DREAMING IN GREEN

You know you're a herper when...

... you've dreamt of serendipitously
finding rare amphibians that
don't actually exist.
—Jolijn de Hoogh,
Meijel, The Netherlands

...you realise it isn't a serpent that you
are looking at, but simply a scaly jewel.
—Jolijn de Hoogh,
Meijel, The Netherlands

You know you're a herper when...

...you actually know that turtles
aren't always slow.

...you sometimes get up in the middle
of the night just to watch
your herps sleep.
—Maria McArther, Caseyville, IL

...you watch the Aldabra tortoises walk
around their enclosure on a nice sunny
day, turn to a friend, and say,
"It's a great day to be a turtle!"

...you fall in love with herps when
you look into their eyes.

You know you're a herper when...

...you start to use
the word "herper."

...you dream in green.
Pam Brzezinski, Mukwonago, WI

You don't know exactly when you
became a herper; it's just something
you've done your whole life.
You couldn't go without herps
at this point; you might as well
lop off an arm.

www.ingramcontent.com/pod-product-compliance
Lightning Source LLC
Chambersburg PA
CBHW031300060726

47590CB00003B/997